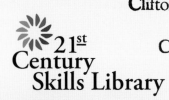

21st
Century
Skills Library

COOL CAREERS

ATHLETIC TRAINER

Patricia K. Kummer

Cherry Lake Publishing
Ann Arbor, Michigan

CHERRY LAKE
Publishing

Published in the United States of America by Cherry Lake Publishing
Ann Arbor, Michigan
www.cherrylakepublishing.com

Content Adviser: Thomas Sawyer, EdD, Professor of Recreation and Sport
Management, Indiana State University

Photo Credits: Cover and pages 1 and 24, ©Steve Skjold/Alamy; pages 4 and 10, ©Jim
West/Alamy; page 6, ©The Print Collector/Alamy; page 8, ©JUPITERIMAGES/Brand
X/Alamy; page 12, ©JUPITERIMAGES/Creatas/Alamy; page 15, ©JUPITERIMAGES/
BananaStock/Alamy; page 16, ©David Young-Wolff/Alamy; page 19, ©Kim Karpeles/
Alamy; page 20, ©iStockphoto.com/ranplett; page 22, ©Design Pics Inc./Alamy; page
26, ©Juergen Hasenkopf/Alamy

Library of Congress Cataloging-in-Publication Data
Kummer, Patricia K.
Athletic trainer / Patricia K. Kummer.
   p. cm.—(Cool careers)
Includes index.
ISBN-13: 978-1-60279-303-3
ISBN-10: 1-60279-303-4
1. Athletic trainers—Juvenile literature. I. Title. II. Series.
GV428.7.K86 2009
617.1'027—dc22   7|3| 2008010475

*Cherry Lake Publishing would like to acknowledge the work of
The Partnership for 21st Century Skills.
Please visit* www.21stcenturyskills.org *for more information.*

TABLE OF CONTENTS

CHAPTER ONE

FROM ANCIENT TIMES TO TODAY

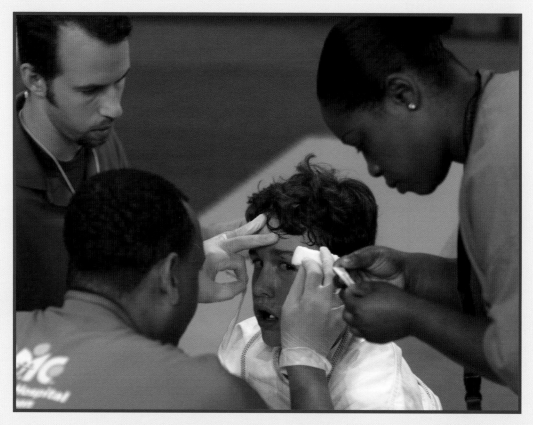

Teamwork is important in the work of an athletic trainer.

A professional basketball player **sprains** her ankle while chasing after the ball. Two college football players crash into each other. One of them falls to the ground with a **concussion**. When these injuries occur, an athletic trainer runs to help the **athlete**. He or she treats the athlete's injuries.

Treating injuries is only a small part of an athletic trainer's job. Athletic trainers also work hard to prevent injuries. They set up exercise programs that help athletes warm up and stretch their muscles. They also help athletes recover from sports injuries. Not all athletic trainers work with professional or college sports teams. Many of them work for high school teams, companies, hospitals, and sports medicine clinics. Some also work with the military or with individual performers.

Athletic trainers have been working with athletes for more than 2,000 years. Some of the early trainers helped athletes prepare for the Olympic Games in ancient Greece. Later, in the Roman Empire, trainers prepared gladiators for matches with each other or

Athletic trainers worked with gladiators in ancient Rome.

with wild animals. Roman trainers also worked with charioteers. These were athletes who raced chariots pulled by teams of horses.

In the mid-1800s, many people in the United States enjoyed taking part in sports. Some U.S. colleges started programs in gymnastics and football. At first, coaches and doctors took care of athletes' injuries. Then a few colleges started hiring special people to train, condition, and care for athletes. Those people were some of the first modern-day athletic trainers. These early trainers did not have college degrees or special training for their jobs. They learned on the job and taught themselves the skills they needed. Sometimes a bucket of cold water and a sponge served as their only first-aid supplies.

In 1916, athletic trainers got help from a book titled *Athletic Training* by Dr. Samuel Bilik. It is believed to be the first book on the subject. Bilik felt that if athletic trainers were properly trained, there would be fewer seriously injured athletes.

In 1932, athletic trainers became part of the staff of the U.S. Olympic team. Five athletic trainers traveled to Los Angeles, California, for the Summer Olympics.

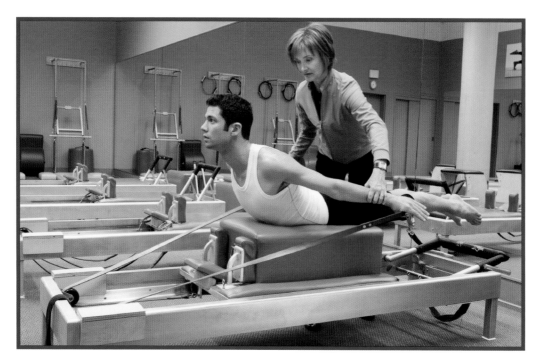

Athletic trainers need to be familiar with many kinds of fitness equipment.

Brothers Frank and Charles "Chuck" Cramer were two of those trainers.

The National Athletic Trainers Association (NATA) was founded in 1950. Members of the newly formed association worked hard to make the career of athletic trainer a respected one. The group pushed for colleges and universities to offer programs that would help instruct athletic trainers. In 1959, the NATA created a list of courses that all athletic trainers should take. In 1969, the American Medical Association (AMA) recognized the importance of the role of the athletic trainer. In 1970, the NATA held the first national certification test. Those who pass the test are known as **certified** athletic trainers. They are the only people who can truly be called athletic trainers. The AMA formally recognized athletic training as a healthcare profession in 1990.

In 2008, about 41,000 certified athletic trainers were working in the United States. The career of athletic trainer is now widely respected.

21st Century Content

Until the 1970s, most athletic trainers were men. In 1972, the U.S. Congress passed a law known as Title IX. Among other things, this law called for high schools and colleges to offer equal sports programs for male and female students. As more girls and women became active in sports, more women became athletic trainers. In 1974, only 10 women were certified as athletic trainers. By 2008, there were about 21,000 female athletic trainers.

CHAPTER TWO

BECOMING AN ATHLETIC TRAINER

Athletic trainers usually wear comfortable clothing.

Do you enjoy being physically active and playing sports? Are you interested in science and how the human body works? Do you like to help people? These are a few of the qualities that an athletic trainer should have.

Working well with many kinds of people is an important skill for athletic trainers. They must be able to tell athletes how to take care of themselves. They have to let coaches know if an athlete is unable to play. Sometimes they may have to explain an athlete's injury to a doctor. To work with all these people, athletic trainers must have good communication skills.

Making good decisions quickly is another skill that athletic trainers should have. When an injury occurs, athletic trainers must decide right away on the best treatment. They also must know if the injury requires a doctor's attention or a trip to the hospital.

Playing and watching sports helps athletic trainers understand the kinds of injuries that can occur. Their first-hand experience helps them teach athletes how to prevent injuries. It also gives them a better understanding of how to treat injuries that do occur.

Having a strong stomach and a strong mind are important qualities, too. Athletic trainers have to be able to face the sight of blood and take care of broken bones. They

It is smart to take extra science classes if you want to become an athletic trainer.

also have to stand up to athletes, coaches, and parents who think athletes can play through their injuries.

Athletic trainers can start preparing for this career in high school. They should take health and science classes, such as biology and chemistry. Some high schools have the Athletic Training Student Aide Program. In this program, student athletic trainers learn basic first aid. They also learn how to perform CPR—the way to revive someone who has stopped breathing. They may work as an assistant to the school's athletic trainer. For example, they may make sure that the team's first-aid kit is well supplied. They may also be responsible for making sure that water is always available for the athletes.

Anyone who wants to become a certified athletic trainer must go to college. There are more than 350 athletic training programs in the United States. This program includes classes in the sciences as well as practical training. Some of these classes are **anatomy, biomechanics, kinetics,** and **physiology**. Other classes include fitness and exercise, nutrition, budgeting, and recordkeeping. Practical training classes include how to identify injuries,

treat injuries, and determine the best **rehabilitation** exercises.

College graduates with a degree in athletic training must take and pass a national certification test. The Board of Certification (BOC), Inc., oversees the certification process.

As of 2006, 35 states required certified athletic trainers to become licensed in their state. In some states, athletic trainers have to take a second test to become licensed. In other states, they can simply show that they passed the BOC certification test.

To remain certified, athletic trainers must receive continuing

Attending conferences gives athletic trainers a chance to meet other professionals in their industry.

education credits (CEUs). Every three years, they must complete 80 hours of medically related CEUs. Many of these credits can be earned by going to special sessions or classes at conferences held each year by various organizations. Writing articles that are published in sports medicine journals can also earn CEUs.

CHAPTER THREE

THE WORK OF AN ATHLETIC TRAINER

Athletic trainers take notes on the types of exercises athletes perform.

Athletic trainers' responsibilities include preventing injuries and identifying and treating injuries. They also direct rehabilitation and keep accurate records. Athletic trainers do several things to prevent injuries. They make sure that athletes do warm-up exercises. The exercises stretch and condition their muscles and joints before practices or competitions. When necessary, athletic trainers also wrap and tape athletes' ankles, wrists, and knees. This helps to prevent sprains and **strains** from pulled **ligaments** and **tendons**. Athletic trainers also encourage athletes to eat healthy foods and to drink plenty of water.

Even with these preventive measures, injuries do happen. The athletic trainer must quickly identify the injury and decide how to treat it. The athletic trainer must also be able to determine when an athlete requires a doctor's care or needs to go to a hospital.

After an injury, a rehabilitation program helps bring the injured athlete back to normal health. When the injuries have healed, athletic trainers help athletes follow a program of special activities and exercises that strengthen the recovering muscles or joints.

Athletic trainers also have to be good managers of paperwork and money. They keep accurate medical records for all their athletes. They stay in contact with

their injured athletes' doctors. The doctors let the athletic trainers know when athletes can resume activity. Athletic trainers are assigned a yearly budget—money that is available for supplies, equipment, and extra staff. They are responsible for ordering and paying for everything that's needed to take care of their athletes.

About 40 percent of athletic trainers work with sports teams in schools or professional settings. About 800 athletic trainers work with professional athletes on baseball, basketball, football, and hockey teams. They also work with professional golfers, tennis players, race-car drivers, and rodeo competitors.

Some athletic trainers work for professional sports teams.

About 34 percent of athletic trainers work in medical clinics and sports medicine centers. In these settings, doctors monitor the work of athletic trainers. These athletic trainers can take medical histories, perform parts of physical examinations, and determine basic injuries.

Athletic trainers make sure that people use exercise equipment correctly.

They can also put on casts and **splints**. They can help patients learn how to use a cane or crutches. All of these actions speed up the healing process for patients. They don't have to wait for an appointment with a doctor. Athletic trainers, however, refer all serious injuries immediately to a doctor. Athletic trainers in medical clinics also spend time helping patients with rehabilitation.

Private companies such as Coca-Cola, FedEx, Frito-Lay, and Nike also hire athletic trainers. Athletic trainers manage injury prevention and rehabilitation programs for employees of these companies. Workers in offices and on assembly lines can have the same kinds of joint and muscle injuries as athletes.

About 20 percent of athletic trainers work at YMCAs, gyms, fitness centers, and health clubs. Athletic trainers show members how to warm up before exercising and how to use weight-training equipment correctly. They also help members with their rehabilitation exercises. If accidents or injuries occur in these settings, athletic trainers can respond immediately.

Two other work settings for athletic trainers include performing arts centers and the military. Performers can experience the same injuries to their joints and muscles as athletes. Ballet companies, Cirque du Soleil, and the

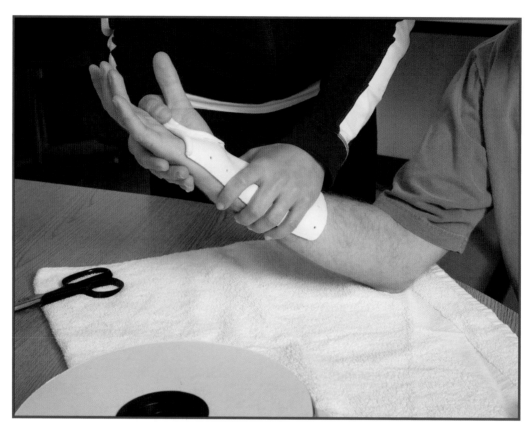

Splints help prevent further damage by keeping injured body parts still.

Radio City Music Hall Rockettes are just some examples of groups with athletic trainers on their staffs. In recent years, many branches of the military service have hired athletic trainers. The trainers have changed the way military recruits are physically trained and conditioned. As a result, injuries during military training have dropped greatly.

Some of the basic supplies that athletic trainers use include tape, wraps, braces, and splints. These supplies help support weak or sore muscles and joints. Cold packs and heat packs are used to bring down swelling or ease the soreness of a strain or sprain. Antiseptics, which remove germs from wounds, and bandages, which protect wounds, are other important supplies.

Athletic trainers must know how to use and operate several kinds of equipment. If athletic trainers think someone's neck or spine might be injured, they carefully move the injured athlete onto a **spine board**. The **whirlpool** helps loosen tight or sore arm, leg, and shoulder muscles. Athletic trainers also guide the use of weight machines for warm-up, conditioning, and rehabilitation exercises. New methods of training are constantly being developed.

CHAPTER FOUR

A LOOK AHEAD FOR ATHLETIC TRAINERS

Athletic trainers need special skills to work with young athletes.

With more people enjoying physical activity and sports, the need for athletic trainers will continue to grow. More medical clinics and hospitals are adding sports medicine departments. Gyms, health clubs, and fitness centers continue to open more sites. All of these medical and health facilities are hiring athletic trainers. More high schools—and even some elementary and middle schools—are hiring athletic trainers. The U.S. Bureau of Labor Statistics expects the number of athletic training jobs to increase by 24 percent by 2016. This is much faster than the expected growth for other occupations.

Jobs in companies are also expected to continue to grow. Employers rely on athletic trainers to organize injury prevention programs and manage

Learning & Innovation Skills

Imagine that you are a member of your town's school board. The athletic director at the high school wants to hire an athletic trainer. The athletic trainer would work with all of the sports teams and students in physical education classes. Some school board members do not want to spend money for an athletic trainer's salary. They do not think that an athletic trainer is needed. They think the coaches and physical education teachers can handle any athletic injuries that happen. How would you vote on this issue? Why? What reasons would you present to persuade the other school board members to vote with you?

Computers are great tools for keeping athletic trainers organized. They can help track an athlete's progress.

any injuries that come up. Their efforts can help reduce employee sick leave and companies' health insurance payments.

Computers will play a bigger role in the way athletic trainers do their jobs. Athletic trainers are becoming increasingly responsible for budgeting and other paperwork. They will need to learn computer programs to handle those responsibilities accurately and efficiently. More of the equipment they use when working with athletes will also be computerized. Good computer skills will help them get the most from the equipment available to them.

Athletic trainers' working hours are expected to increase because the number of patients is predicted to rise. Currently, those working in hospitals and clinics work 40 to 50 hours a week. They usually have evenings and weekends off. Athletic trainers in schools sometimes work 50 to 60 hours a week. They might also work six or seven days a week because teams play or practice on weekends and evenings. Athletic trainers for professional teams work

12 hours a day during training camps and on practice and game days.

The salaries for athletic trainers are expected to increase slowly. The yearly salary range differs according to work setting and responsibility. The average salary for athletic trainers in health and fitness centers is about $38,000; in a clinic, about $41,000; and in a company setting, about $44,000. Athletic trainers in schools earn from $25,000 to $35,000. Those who have master's degrees and work in colleges can earn up to $60,000. Athletic trainers with professional sports teams can earn from $60,000 to $125,000.

A career as an athletic trainer can be exciting and rewarding. There are opportunities to help keep people fit in many different kinds of settings. For sports lovers with a real interest in how the human body works, it might just be a winning career!

Some Famous Athletic Trainers

Dr. Samuel E. Bilik (1890–?) is known as the Father of Athletic Training. He published *Athletic Training* in 1916 and *The Trainer's Bible* in 1917. In the 1920s, he started teaching classes for athletic trainers. He also founded an athletic supply company. He was inducted into the NATA Hall of Fame in 1962.

Charles "Chuck" Cramer (1892–1984) and Frank Cramer (1888–1971) were brothers who were among the first athletic trainers for the U.S. Olympic team in 1932. Both men were founding members of the NATA. In 1962, both Chuck and Frank were inducted into the NATA Hall of Fame.

Julie Max (1953–) served as the first female president of the NATA (2000–2004). She has been part of the University of California at Fullerton's athletic training department since 1979 and has served as the head athletic trainer since 1990. She also teaches kinesiology courses there. In 2007, she was inducted into the NATA Hall of Fame.

William E. "Pinky" Newell (1924–1984) from Enid, Oklahoma, is known as the Father of Modern Athletic Training. He held the position of head athletic trainer of Purdue University from 1950 to 1977. In 1972, he was inducted into the NATA Hall of Fame. He served as an athletic trainer for the U.S. Olympic teams at the 1976 Summer Games in Montreal, Canada, and at the 1980 Winter Games in Lake Placid, New York.

Gail Weldon (1951–1991) was a pioneer in helping women in the field of athletic training. In 1974, she was one of the first 10 women to be certified as athletic trainers. In 1976, she was the first female athletic trainer selected to serve on the U.S. Olympic team's medical staff. In 1995, she was the first woman elected to the NATA Hall of Fame. Each year, the NATA honors a female athletic trainer with the Gail Weldon Visionary Award.

GLOSSARY

anatomy (uh-NAT-uh-mee) the science of how the human body is organized

athlete (ATH-leet) a person who is skilled at playing a sport or sports

biomechanics (bye-oh-muh-KAN-iks) the study of how the body's musculoskeletal system works

certified (SUR-tuh-fyed) officially approved to be able to do a job, usually after passing a test

concussion (kuhn-KUSH-uhn) an injury to the brain from a blow to the head that can cause a person to become dizzy or lose consciousness

kinetics (ki-NET-iks) the study of how parts of the body move

ligaments (LIG-uh-muhntz) thick bands of tissue that connect one bone to another bone

physiology (fih-zee-AH-luh-gee) the study of the activities of the body's tissues and cells

rehabilitation (ree-uh-bi-luh-TAY-shuhn) special activities, exercises, or other programs that return an athlete to normal health after an injury

spine board (SPINE BORD) a specially designed board used to prevent an injured person's spine from moving

splints (SPLINTZ) pieces of wood, plastic, or metal used to prevent movement of a joint or to support an injured arm or leg

sprains (SPRAYNZ) stretches or tears a ligament

strains (STRAYNZ) stretches or tears of a muscle or tendon

tendons (TEN-duhnz) thick bands of tissue that connect a muscle to a bone

whirlpool (WURL-pool) a tub in which jets of air circulate hot or cold water

For More Information

Books

Field, Shelly. *Career Opportunities in the Sports Industry.*
3rd ed. New York: Ferguson Publishing, 2004.

Heitzmann, William Ray. *Careers for Sports Nuts and Other
Athletic Types.* Chicago: McGraw Hill, 2004.

Reeves, Diane Lindsey, Lindsey Clasen, and Nancy Bond (illustrator). *Career
Ideas for Kids Who Like Sports.* New York: Checkmark Books, 2007.

Web Sites

MCHS Athletic Training Student Aide Program
www.mchs.net/sports/sportspage/athletic_training/index.html
Find out about one school's Athletic Training Student Aide Program

National Athletic Trainers' Association
www.nata.org
Links to NATA's Hall of Fame, professional journal, recent research,
and regional and state athletic trainers' associations

INDEX

ABOUT THE AUTHOR

Patricia K. Kummer has written more than 60 children's nonfiction books on a variety of topics. Many of her books have been about the states, other countries, natural wonders, and inventions. She also wrote *Sports Medicine Doctor* in the Cool Careers series. Ms. Kummer likes researching and writing nonfiction because she knows truth is stranger than fiction! Besides writing, she teaches adults about writing nonfiction for children and visits schools, where she enjoys talking to children about the writing process. When she is not working, Ms. Kummer likes to read and to travel.